STARVING THE ANGER GREMLIN

ANGER MANAGEMENT FOR YOUNG PEOPLE

Kate Collins-Donnelly

Trafford
PUBLISHING

Thank you to all the children who allowed me to use their artwork

Order this book online at www.trafford.com/07-0628
or email orders@trafford.com

Most Trafford titles are also available at major online book retailers.

© Copyright 2007 Kate Collins-Donnelly.
Cover design by YODA

Note for Librarians: A cataloguing record for this book is available from Library and Archives Canada at www.collectionscanada.ca/amicus/index-e.html

ISBN: 978-1-4251-2227-0

We at Trafford believe that it is the responsibility of us all, as both individuals and corporations, to make choices that are environmentally and socially sound. You, in turn, are supporting this responsible conduct each time you purchase a Trafford book, or make use of our publishing services. To find out how you are helping, please visit www.trafford.com/responsiblepublishing.html

Our mission is to efficiently provide the world's finest, most comprehensive book publishing service, enabling every author to experience success. To find out how to publish your book, your way, and have it available worldwide, visit us online at www.trafford.com/10510

Trafford PUBLISHING™ www.trafford.com

North America & international
toll-free: 1 888 232 4444 (USA & Canada)
phone: 250 383 6864 ♦ fax: 250 383 6804 ♦ email: info@trafford.com

The United Kingdom & Europe
phone: +44 (0)1865 722 113 ♦ local rate: 0845 230 9601
facsimile: +44 (0)1865 722 868 ♦ email: info.uk@trafford.com

10 9 8 7 6 5 4 3 2 1

CONTENTS

Starving the Anger Gremlin

ABOUT THE AUTHOR

Hi I'm Kate and I'm a psychologist, therapist and anger management consultant. I have considerable experience of working with young people on a wide range of different issues, including anger, and also with parents and professionals on how to teach anger management skills to young people.

The need for a book on anger management aimed at young people themselves became evident through this work. This book is about teaching young people to help themselves by learning about the basics of anger and how to control it, but in an interesting and easily accessible way. The approach that this book takes has been tried and tested with many young people since I began my career. Some of these young people have in fact contributed their stories, their thoughts and their drawings to this book in order to help others to learn how to control their anger like they have.

In a nutshell, I want to spread the word far and wide on how to manage your anger, but in a simple, activity-filled, easily readable and interesting way. I hope my book achieves this. I'll let you be the judge.

Happy reading!

Kate

ACKNOWLEDGEMENTS

Thank you to the colleagues that have dedicated their time, positivity, comments and support to this project. A special thank you goes to Maria for her advice, knowledge and unwavering support as well as her absolute belief in what I was trying to achieve through this book. And last, but by no means least, I would like to thank all the young people who I have worked with and learnt from, especially those who were brave enough to share their stories in order to help others.

Starving the Anger Gremlin

INTRODUCTION

If you answered yes to any of the above, then this book is here to help you!

It contains information and activities, as well as comments from other young people, in order to help you to control your anger and express it in more positive ways. It really is possible!

BUT REMEMBER…. Starting to explore your anger may well raise some really difficult issues for you. So it's important that you can talk to someone you trust about these issues, such as a parent, relative, friend, teacher or counsellor. Part of getting control back is being able to share how you feel with someone else.

WHAT IS ANGER?

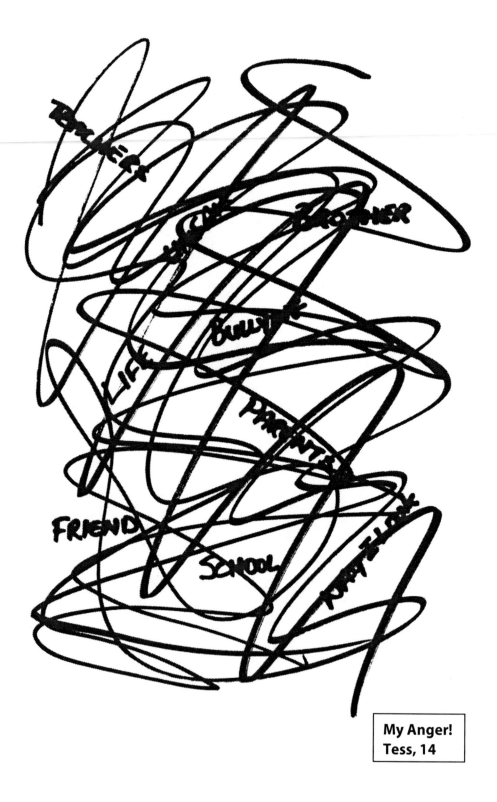

My Anger!
Tess, 14

Anger is an important emotion that is normal and natural when used with control. We all get angry.

Anger helps us to cope with:

- Threats
- Hurt (e.g. if our rights are being violated)
- Frustration (e.g. if we feel our basic needs aren't being met)

So anger can be positive if expressed in the right way.

Where anger becomes a problem is if it:

- Is displayed too frequently
- Interferes with aspects of your life (e.g. relationships, school or work)
- Is used as a tool to get what you want (e.g. if a child realises that he or she gets attention from his or her Mum if he or she throws a tantrum)
- Is displayed aggressively (e.g. fighting, shouting, threatening)
- Turned against yourself
- Buried inside and bottled up
- Taken out on someone else

Here are some quotes from other young people on their problematic angry behaviours.

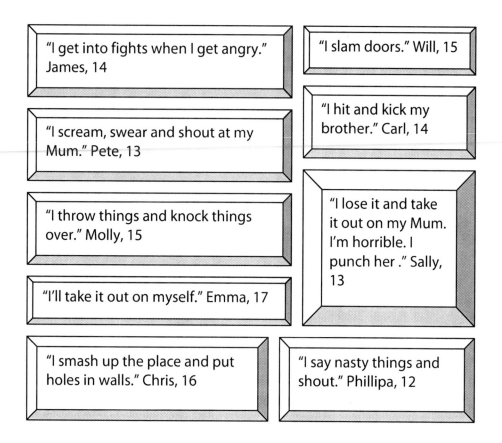

"I get into fights when I get angry." James, 14

"I slam doors." Will, 15

"I scream, swear and shout at my Mum." Pete, 13

"I hit and kick my brother." Carl, 14

"I throw things and knock things over." Molly, 15

"I lose it and take it out on my Mum. I'm horrible. I punch her ." Sally, 13

"I'll take it out on myself." Emma, 17

"I smash up the place and put holes in walls." Chris, 16

"I say nasty things and shout." Phillipa, 12

Do any of these sound familiar?

Don't worry if they do. By understanding more about your anger and by learning how to manage it and express it constructively, your experiences of anger can become more positive!

MY ANGER

Let's start exploring your anger using the My Anger Questionnaire.

MY ANGER QUESTIONNAIRE

1. How often do you get angry? Circle your answer

a) Often   b) Sometimes   c) Rarely   d) Never

2. Think about how you tend to feel physically when you get angry. Circle which of the following applies to you.

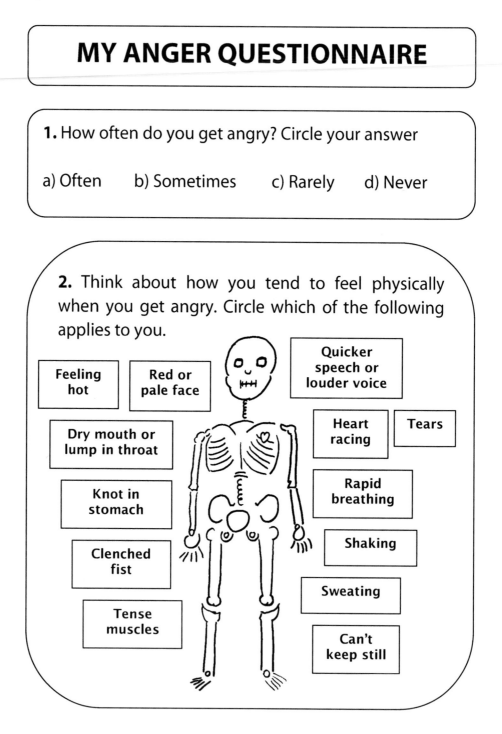

Feeling hot

Red or pale face

Quicker speech or louder voice

Dry mouth or lump in throat

Heart racing

Tears

Knot in stomach

Rapid breathing

Clenched fist

Shaking

Sweating

Tense muscles

Can't keep still

3. Below are different ways that people can react when they get angry. Tick any that apply to you when you get angry from both groups A and B.

GROUP A BEHAVIOURS		
Threaten	Shove	
Shout	Accuse or blame	
Slam doors	Throw things	
Criticise myself	Verbally abuse	
Punch	Break things	
Swear	Cry	
Make sly digs	Lose control	
Kick	Get angry with self	
Bully	Bottle anger up	
Start vicious rumours	Use a weapon	
Get revenge	Become cold	
Hurt myself	Behave recklessly	
Throw a tantrum	Silent treatment	
Snap at people	Say nasty things	
Other	Other	
GROUP B BEHAVIOURS		
Talk to someone	Distract myself	
Calm myself down	Walk away	
Count to 10	Write down feelings	
Ignore it	Other.................	

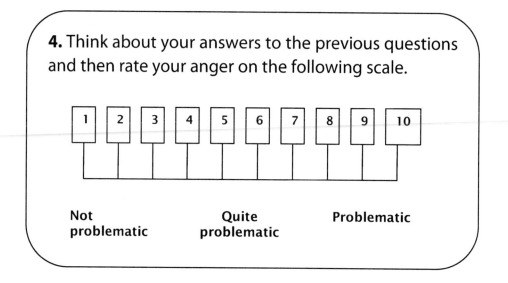

4. Think about your answers to the previous questions and then rate your anger on the following scale.

| 1 | 2 | 3 | 4 | 5 | 6 | 7 | 8 | 9 | 10 |

Not problematic   **Quite problematic**   **Problematic**

Problematic Anger

If you have scored your anger as problematic on the scale it's probably because you are getting angry a lot and experiencing several physical symptoms when you get angry (we will look at the effects this has on your physical health in chapter eight). It's also probably because most of your angry behaviours fall into the Group A Behaviours in question three.

Q. Do you see any other patterns in your angry behaviours?

Are you particularly **aggressive**, such as throwing things, punching, kicking, verbally abusing, using a weapon, etc.?

Perhaps you **turn it inwards** – i.e. direct it at yourself? Examples of this include self-criticism and self-harming.

Or do you tend to try and bottle up your anger? This is known as **suppressing** your anger.

Or perhaps you direct it at other people, instead of those who you feel have triggered your anger? This is known as **displaced** anger. For example, if you are angry because your Mum has told you that you are grounded, but instead of expressing that anger towards your Mum, you shout at your sister.

Now you have a general picture of what your anger tends to be like we can start to look at how and why your anger occurs, the effects it has, and how to control it.

HOW DOES ANGER OCCUR?

What makes you angry?

List anything that makes you angry in your Anger Box below.

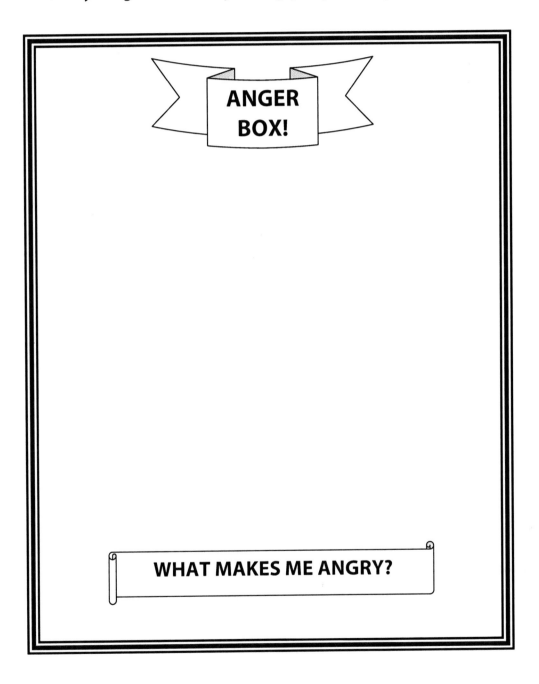

Your list may include:

People (e.g. brother)
Pets
Places (e.g. school)
Situations / events
(e.g. the arguments
between your parents)
Someone's actions (e.g.
your Mum telling you
off)
Someone's attitude
(e.g. a person's racist
attitude)

These are all examples of the types of things that people list when asked what makes them angry.

However, these only trigger an angry reaction. They DO NOT cause it.

Let's see what we mean by thinking about the following question.

Q. When your PE teacher doesn't pick you for the school team you get angry. Is your teacher controlling your anger?

YES   or   NO

Q. If your answer is 'yes,' does that mean she has an anger remote control that she is pointing at you?

YES   or   NO

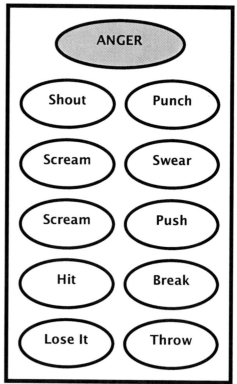

Q. Is she pressing a big **ANGER** button that is causing you to get angry?

YES   or   NO

A. The answers to all three questions are actually **NO!** Your teacher isn't pressing an anger button on a remote control to make you angry. She isn't controlling your anger at all.

Q. So who **IS** in control of your anger?

YOU   or   THE CHILDREN WHO WERE PICKED FOR THE TEAM

A. The answer is **YOU!** The remote control is in **YOUR** hands!

It's **YOUR** thoughts and beliefs that make you angry. Anger is about how **YOU** react to a situation not the situation itself.

YOU'RE THE ONE IN CONTROL OF YOUR ANGER!

Let's have a look at some examples to see what I mean.

Example 1

Your Dad is supposed to come to watch you in the school play, but he doesn't turn up. You think to yourself:

- 'He could've let me know.'
- 'He's obviously had a better offer.'
- 'He's probably stuck at work again.'
- 'I knew he wasn't really interested.'

Rate how angry you think you'd be on the scale overleaf.

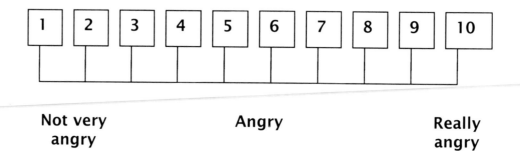

Not very angry   **Angry**   **Really angry**

Ok now imagine that when you get home you find out that your Dad had fallen over, broken his leg and had spent the evening at the hospital.

Now how angry would you be on a scale of 1 to 10?

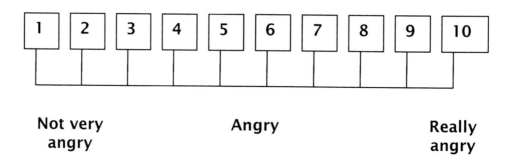

Not very angry   **Angry**   **Really angry**

Q. Did you rate your anger as higher or lower than before?

Higher   or   Lower

Let's have a look at another example.

Example 2

You work as a shop assistant at weekends and one day the boss asks you to create a display of tinned foods that are on offer. You've just finished balancing the last can when someone crashes into your display and sends the cans flying! How angry would you be on a scale of one to ten?

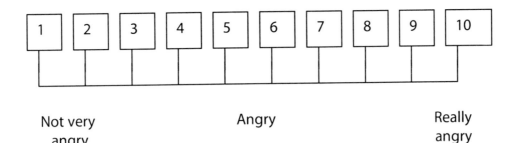

Not very   Angry   Really
angry   angry

But let's say the person that has fallen into your display had tripped on something that had been spilt on the floor. How would you rate your anger now?

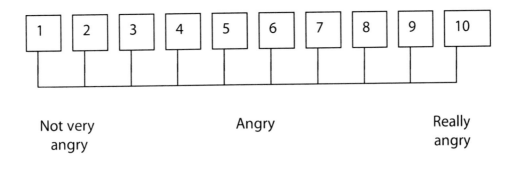

Not very   Angry   Really
angry   angry

Q. Did you rate your anger as higher or lower than before?

Higher   or   Lower

A. I'm sure that in both examples you were less angry in the second version of the story than the first.

Q. So what is it that makes you less angry?

A. The answer is you!

It's not the situation itself that controls your level of anger. If it was, we would all react in the same ways in the same situations.   However, we don't. Reactions differ from individual to individual.

Q. So if it's not the situation itself that determines your level of anger and type of angry reaction what is it?

A. It's how **you think** about the situation.

For example, if you instantly assume that the person knocked over your display on purpose, your thoughts would be triggering your angry reaction. However, if you initially thought that it might have been an accident, your thoughts would probably trigger a less angry reaction.

So you **can** control how you react.

You're the one in control of your anger!

ANGER CONTROL

Ok so you are the one who is in control of how you act when you get angry. But your ability to control your anger at any given point in time can also be affected by other factors. The following task will help you to work out what these factors are. Firstly read through the different scenarios below.

Scenario 1
Mary is 6. Her dad loses his temper all the time and often punches the wall and kicks things. Mary has been getting into a lot of trouble at school recently because when she gets mad or upset over something she hits someone.

Scenario 2
Sam is 16. Whenever Sam wants something he will shout and verbally abuse his parents until he gets it.

Scenario 3
Tim is 13. His parents believe that homosexuality is a sin. Tim finds out his brother is gay. He loses it and starts a fight with him.

Scenario 4
Sarah is 17. She works three jobs in order to pay her rent and can't afford to take time off. One evening she is on her way home from work and is really tired. Someone bumps into her in the street. She shouts at them and pushes them back.

Scenario 5
Dave is 18. He's just found out that his girlfriend cheated on him with his best mate. That same day Dave is told by his college tutor that his essay wasn't good enough. Dave throws the essay at his tutor, storms out of the office and slams the door.

Now I want you to think about what might be affecting each person's anger control in each of the different scenarios.
See if you can match up the scenario number below with the factor affecting the person's anger control in that scenario.

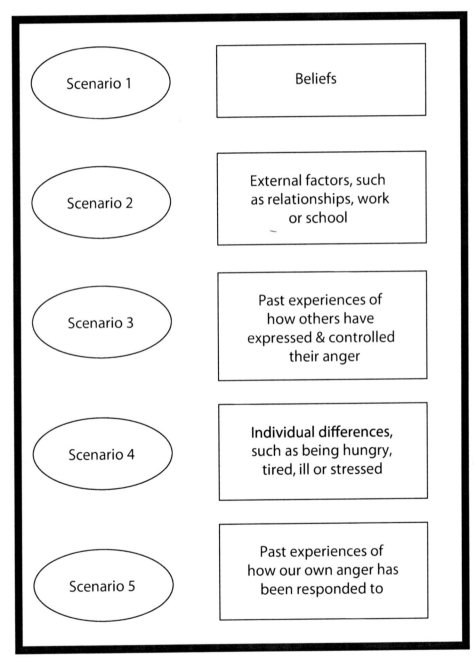

You will find the answers to this 'match the scenarios' task on page 76.

As you can see a person can develop a habit of reacting in a certain way when they get angry because of their **past experiences.** We learn from what we see and experience. So we learn from how we see other people acting when they get angry and from how other people respond to our own angry outbursts.

But how a person tends to react can also change depending upon the particular **individual and external circumstances** at that point in time, such as being ill or tired or having experienced a relationship break-up, etc.

But although these things impact on our anger control, they **don't stop us** from being in control of our anger. We cannot use them as excuses.

We are still in control of how we react.

So even when we have a right to be angry (for example, if we are being bullied at school) we cannot react in negative ways, such as taking our anger out on someone else.

So how are we supposed to control and express our anger?

Well let's start by looking at the interaction between **"the trigger situation and your angry reaction"** in more detail.

SUMMING UP!

We've now gone through all the methods you need to get your anger under control. It's now down to you to put them into practice.

Only you can change how you react.

It's YOU that's in control of your anger!

You have all the power!

So let's have a quick recap before we finish.

Write down five things that you have learnt about your anger and how to control it in your anger box below.

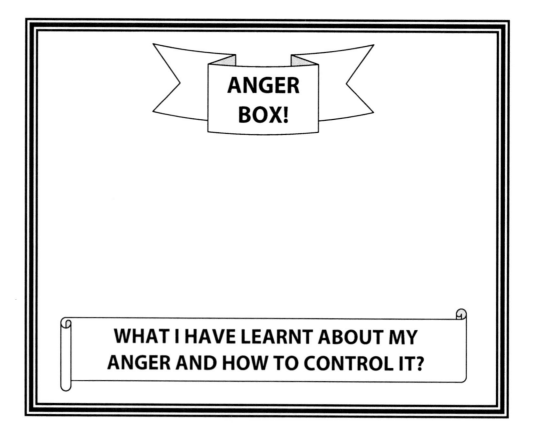

ANGER QUIZ

OK, let's test what you've learnt in the Anger Quiz!

1. Sam is 15. He is late getting to school as his Mum's car had a flat tyre. His teacher tells him not to be late again. Sam swears at the teacher and kicks a chair.

Who is in control of Sam's anger?

a) Sam   b) Sam's teacher   c) Sam's Mum

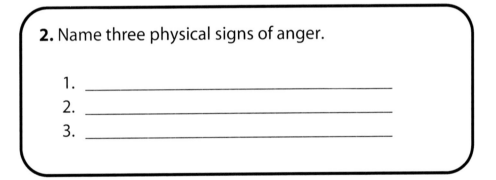

2. Name three physical signs of anger.

1. _____
2. _____
3. _____

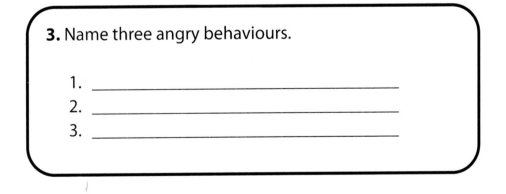

3. Name three angry behaviours.

1. _____
2. _____
3. _____

4. Which of the following can affect your anger control?

a) your past experiences of how other people react when they get angry
b) stress
c) your past experiences of how others have reacted to your anger
d) tiredness
e) all of the above

5. Jane is 14. Her boyfriend had been cheating on her with her best friend Sarah. Jane punched Sarah.

Who is in control of Jane's anger?

a) Jane   b) Jane's boyfriend   c) Sarah

6. Jason is 21. He used to get suspended from school a lot for getting into fights. Now, he gets into rows all the time over silly little things at work. Name two ways in which Jason's anger might be affecting him.

1. _____

2. _____

7. Beth is 16 and very angry. Yesterday, she got into a fight and smashed the window on someone's car. Beth's mum had to miss a day's work to collect Beth from the police station. Beth is being charged with criminal damage. Beth's mum isn't sleeping very well and is snapping at everyone all the time. Name two ways in which Beth's anger has affected her mum.

1. _____

2. _____

8. What do you need to do to the Anger Gremlin?

a) Feed it   b) Starve it

9. Name two ways to control your anger.

1. _____

2. _____

10. Identify one question you should ask yourself when you begin to get angry.

1. _____

11. If you want to express your anger positively, name two things that you could do.

     1. _____

     2. _____

12. If you want to express your anger positively, name two things that you shouldn't do.

     1. _____

     2. _____

13. Who is in control of your anger?

a) Something   b) Someone   c) You

Turn to page 76 to see how you've got on!

Well done! I'm sure you did fantastically!

Finally, let's check on what you think your anger is like now. Do you remember the My Anger Questionnaire? Well now I want you to complete the questionnaire again.

MY ANGER QUESTIONNAIRE

1. How often do you get angry? Circle your answer

a) Often   b) Sometimes   c) Rarely   d) Never

2. Think about how you tend to feel physically when you get angry. Circle which of the following applies to you.

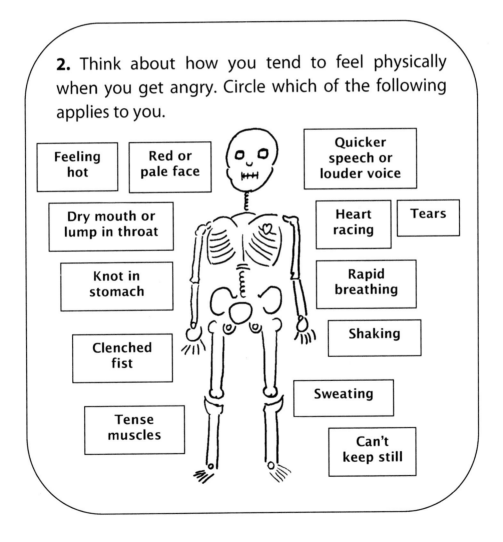

Feeling hot

Red or pale face

Quicker speech or louder voice

Dry mouth or lump in throat

Heart racing

Tears

Knot in stomach

Rapid breathing

Clenched fist

Shaking

Sweating

Tense muscles

Can't keep still

3. Below are different ways that people can react when they get angry. Tick any that apply to you when you get angry from both groups A and B.

GROUP A BEHAVIOURS		
Threaten	Shove	
Shout	Accuse or blame	
Slam doors	Throw things	
Criticise myself	Verbally abuse	
Punch	Break things	
Swear	Cry	
Make sly digs	Lose control	
Kick	Get angry with self	
Bully	Bottle anger up	
Start vicious rumours	Use a weapon	
Get revenge	Become cold	
Hurt myself	Behave recklessly	
Throw a tantrum	Silent treatment	
Snap at people	Say nasty things	
Other	Other	
GROUP B BEHAVIOURS		
Talk to someone	Distract myself	
Calm myself down	Walk away	
Count to 10	Write down feelings	
Ignore it	Other.................	

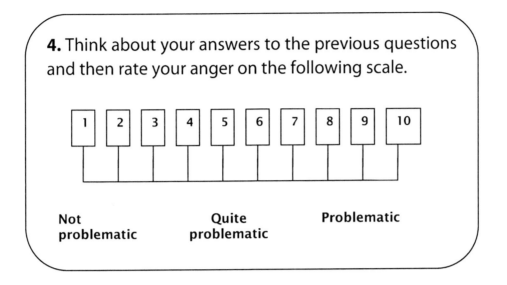

4. Think about your answers to the previous questions and then rate your anger on the following scale.

| 1 | 2 | 3 | 4 | 5 | 6 | 7 | 8 | 9 | 10 |

Not problematic   **Quite problematic**   **Problematic**

Q. Have you seen any changes in your anger since you filled these questions out at the start of the book? If so, what changes have you seen?

A.

_____

_____

Hopefully you've seen your understanding of your anger improve as well as your understanding of how to control it.

As you continue to put everything you have learnt from this book into practice, occasionally ask yourselves the questions in the My Anger Questionnaire to monitor how far you've progressed and how well you're starving your Anger Gremlin!

That's it guys. All the tools you need to control your anger and express it in the right ways are in this book. Now all you have to do is put them into practice.

And remember:

You have a right to be angry at times.

Anger is a normal emotion.

**But you're in control of how you
react when you get angry.**

Positive reactions produce positive results!

And negative reactions produce negative results!

YOU ARE IN CONTROL OF YOUR ANGER!

YOU CAN DO IT!

APPENDICES

ALTERNATIVE THOUGHTS

Anger trigger

What I was thinking?

Alternative thoughts?

Which thoughts are more realistic and why?

Which feed and which starve the Gremlin?

ANGER DIARY

DATE **1.11.19**

I GOT ANGRY TODAY BECAUSE...... I could not find my phone charger

HOW I REACTED

I ignored it.

WHAT WERE THE CONSEQUENCES?

non

DID YOU:

STARVE THE ANGER GREMLIN – YIPEE!	OR	FEED THE ANGER GREMLIN – POO!
Starve		

IF YOU FED HIM, WHAT COULD YOU HAVE DONE DIFFERENTLY THAT WOULD HAVE STARVED HIM?

WOULD THE CONSEQUENCES HAVE BEEN BETTER?

ANSWERS

Anger Quiz

1. (a) Sam
2. See chapter 2
3. See chapter 3
4. (e) All of the above
5. (a) Jane
6. See chapter 8
7. See chapter 8

8. (b) Starve it!
9. See chapter 6
10. See chapter 6
11. See chapter 6
12. See chapter 7
13. (c) You!

Match the Scenarios

Scenario 1 = Past experiences of how others have expressed and controlled their anger.

Scenario 2 = Past experiences of how our own anger has been responded to.

Scenario 3 = Beliefs.

Scenario 4 = Individual differences, such as being hungry, tired, ill or stressed.

Scenario 5 = External factors, such as relationships, work or school.

Printed in the United Kingdom by
Lightning Source UK Ltd., Milton Keynes
138838UK00001B/30/A